The author would like to thank the many people who
have helped with this book, with special thanks to
J. A. Mayoss, David Taylor and Hazel Underwood.
First American Edition
© 1986 by Jane Miller
Published in the United States by Prentice-Hall Books for Young Readers, New York.
Originally published in Great Britain 1986 by
J. M. Dent and Sons Ltd, London, England
Printed and Bound in Italy
Library of Congress Cataloging-in-Publication Data
Miller, Jane, 1925–
  Seasons on the farm.
  Summary: Text and photographs describe farm
activities and animals throughut the four seasons.
  1. Farm life — Juvenile literature. 2. Farms —
Juvenile literature. 3. Seasons — Juvenile literature.
[1. Farm life. 2. Seasons] I. Title.
S519.M55 1986   630   85-28185
ISBN 0-13-797275-X

For Lizzie and Annie

SEASONS ON THE FARM
Jane Miller

Prentice-Hall Books for Young Readers
New York

SPRING

It is spring – a new season of the year. On the farm lambing time has begun. Three lambs have just been born in the barn. Big bales of straw shelter them from the cold wind.

In the field the ewe feeds her lambs with milk from her udder.

Patiently, a sheepdog waits to bring back the sheep.

After the chick has hatched from the egg, the hen will keep it warm under her breast-feathers.

This hen has hatched a goose's egg. She may not know that her baby is a gosling and not a chicken!

Goslings cluster round their mother by a pond. The Canada goose stretches out a wing to shelter her young.

A mare grazes in the field with her long-legged foal. These shire horses work on the farm, pulling ploughs and carts.

In the spring, flowers bloom after the winter cold. Primroses, bluebells and red campion grow in flower gardens

Ducks waddle about finding slugs, snails and insects to eat amongst the daffodils

SUMMER

Now it is summer, and time to pick ripe strawberries. How tempting they are.

The Jersey bull with a ring in his nose strides into the yard. He is as fierce as he sometimes looks!

Out in the field, the sow has given birth to her second litter of piglets this year. Can you see all eight of them sucking her milk? Piglets squeal loudly and greedily at feeding time.

The farmer is cutting grass to make hay to feed his animals.

This grass will be made into silage for the cattle to eat in winter.

In late summer wheat and barley are ripe for harvesting. The combine harvester is drive back and forth through the fields.
It cuts and threshes as it move: along. Threshing separates the grain from the straw.

The baler rolls up the straw and ties it into large, round bales.

A truckload of bales is ready be transported.

You can see the grain pouring out of the spout into the trailer.

AUTUMN

It is autumn and the fruit is ripe in the orchard. The farmer must pick the apples before the frosts begin.

A cat's job is to catch the mice that eat the corn.

Many calves are born in the autumn. This Jersey cow is nuzzling her new calf.

After harvesting, the fields are ploughed.

Then the tractor pulls a seed-drill through the fields, sowing the seed for next year's crop.

A few farmers still plough their land the old way, using horses instead of a tractor.

Many birds prepare to migrate for the winter. The swallows and house martins mass together, perching o the telegraph wires before they fly away to warmer countries.

The geese march around the farm. They are being fattened for Christmas.

In the beechwoods the leaves turn red and gold.

WINTER

Finally it is winter. Animals grow shaggy coats to keep themselves warm. The ponies are given hay when grass is scarce.

A spaniel shelters inside the tractor, waiting for the driver.

Seeing the bright sun, a sow grunts and pokes out her snout.

Working on a farm is not always fun. The tractor crunches through the mud and ice, carting straw for the animals' bedding.

Wild ducks have a hard time finding food when ponds are frozen

In cold weather, cows live in the barn

Ponies wait for the snow to thaw so that they can graze again.

In the woods a hen pheasant searches for food.

A little bird perches on a bud in the garden. He knows that spring is not far away.